Grounding Children in Routines and Procedures for Meaningful Learning

Book 1 of 3 in the series
LITERATE DAYS: READING AND WRITING WITH PRESCHOOL AND PRIMARY CHILDREN

 Gretchen Owocki

Photographer: David Stirling

The author and publisher wish to thank those who have generously given permission to reprint borrowed materials.

Post-it® is a registered trademark of the 3M Company.

Cheerios® is a registered trademark of General Mills, Inc.

Batman® is a registered trademark of DC Comics.

Wikki Stix® is registered trademark of Omnicor, Inc.

Play-Doh® is registered trademark of Hasbro, Inc.

*first*hand

An imprint of Heinemann
A division of Reed Elsevier Inc.
361 Hanover Street
Portsmouth, NH 03801-3912
firsthand.heinemann.com

Offices and agents throughout the world

Library of Congress Catalog-in-Publication Data
CIP data on file with the Library of Congress

ISBN-10: 0-325-01205-9
ISBN-13: 978-0-325-01205-6

Printed in the United States of America on acid-free paper

11 10 09 08 07 ML 1 2 3 4 5 6

Table of Contents

LITERATE DAYS: READING AND WRITING WITH PRESCHOOL AND PRIMARY CHILDREN

PAGE

The Morning Circle Routine:
Focusing on What Matters

CONSIDER THE RESEARCH: Because young children enter school having varied understandings of and experiences with school-related literacy practices (such as sitting for a read-aloud or sharing in the oral reading of a rhyme), they benefit when teachers explicitly show them what is expected as they participate in such practices. Effective teaching mixes *immersion* in the community of practice with *scaffolding* that focuses learners on key patterns of that practice. The more consciously familiar your students become with the patterns of literacy use and the expectations for literacy practices in your classroom, the more independent and successful they can become in that setting (Gee 2000).

Teach this lesson to familiarize children with the routines and expectations for circle time. Suggested circle activities include:

- a greeting
- a calendar review of the day's activities
- shared reading
- a teacher read-aloud.

Circle Time Routine

1. Greeting

2. Calendar

3. Shared Reading

4. Read-Aloud

Form 1.1
Classroom Visual: Circle Time Routine

PREPARATION

After a few days of explicitly working through the routine described here, begin to take the shared reading and teacher read-aloud instruction into more depth, using Lessons 2 and 3.

Circle time guidelines for first weeks of school
Preschool: Up to 15 minutes
Kindergarten: 15 to 20 minutes
First Grade: 20 minutes

- Prepare Form 1.1 to use as a visual. Or take a photograph of a student engaged in each activity and use the photographs for visuals.

- For each circle time, have ready each of the following:

  - A song to call the children together *(such as We're ready for the day./We're ready for the day./Heigh-ho the derry-oh./We're ready for the day or Heigh-ho, heigh-ho./It's off to learn we go…)*
  - A calendar annotated with special events such as children's birthdays, special celebrations, music class, physical education class, and special visitors.
  - A short text to be used for shared reading and placed on an easel if possible. Start the school year with very short rhymes so that children can memorize them and thereby gain confidence in the notion that they can read. Nursery rhymes of four to eight lines work well. (See Lesson 2 for enlarged versions of some beginning texts to try.) Typically, the same text is used for shared reading over the course of three to five days.
  - A text to be used for comprehension instruction/launching the daily reading workshop. Use engaging text from the start. Look for literature that is likely to lead to higher-level thinking and discussion.

- Display the two pieces of text on an easel at your side.

Note to preschool and kindergarten teachers: Early in the year, some children will not sit easily or attentively for circle time. Rather than redirecting these children several times, provide them with a planned alternative activity. This will allow you to sensitively support them over the course of time to adapt to the circle experience. The alternative activity should not be seen by the children as a punishment, but as a temporary haven that respects some children's need for extended support. Suggested alternative activities: Play-Doh, book bin, or drawing.

INTRODUCTION

"Good morning. Every day, we're going to meet right here first thing in the morning. I will let you know that it's time to come here by singing a song." *[Sing together the song that you will use to start the year.]*

"This group time is going to be an important learning time, so it will help if you know just what to do. Today I will talk with you about the routine we'll follow each day."

MODELING AND SCAFFOLDING

Hang Form 1.1 in the meeting area and refer to it for each component of the modeling.

"The first thing to do is **greet** the people next to you. There are lots of ways you could greet someone; let me show you one. *[Greet the child to your immediate left and right.]* "Hello, _____. How are you today?" *[Coach the two students to respond and return the question.]*

"As soon as you are finished with your greeting, sit very quietly and look at me so I'll know you are finished. Let's all try it right now. Greet the people next to you and then look quietly at me.

"Now, does anyone have anything remarkable to share before we begin?" *[Pose this question to the class daily. At first, prompt their responses, encouraging them to share important events in their lives.]*

Children Who Don't Seem Engaged	Possible Reasons	Strategies for Improvement

Form 1.2 Kidwatching Tool: Circle Time Notes

Form 1.2
Kidwatching Tool: Circle Time Notes

kidWATCHING:

Use Form 1.2 to organize your observations and develop strategies for improvement as needed.

Refer to Form 1.1.

" Next we'll check the **calendar** for special events. Today is _____. *[Show how to find the day on the calendar.]* Special events for today are _____.

Refer to Form 1.1.

" **Shared reading** is next. *[Hold up the text.]* That's when we read *together*. I will always sit here and hold the text like this or have the text on this easel. If you're comfortable sitting flat so that kids behind you can see, and you like being close to the book, you could sit near the front. If you like to sit on your knees or feet, and don't mind being a little further from the book, the sides or back would work for you. Go ahead and find a place. Tomorrow, just sit in the place you are right now when you come over."

" Now, let me read to you first and then we will all read together." *[Introduce the text and read it aloud 1-2 times, depending on length. Discuss the content as appropriate. Then read with the class, encouraging all children to "join in as you can."]*

Refer to Form 1.1.

" The **read-aloud** is next. *[Hold up the text.]* Here, you listen and enjoy. If you want to say something about the book while I am reading, signal with a finger *[show]* and I will stop so that we may talk." *[Introduce the text and read it aloud, encouraging discussion. From day one, encourage conversation and high-level thinking rather than a back-and-forth series of teacher questions that have one right answer.]*

CLOSURE

"When we read or listen to books, it helps us **learn** when we think and talk about them like we just did. What did you learn today? What was it like to follow our routines?" *[Refer to Form 1.1.]*

EXTENSION

Over the course of the year, support children in exploring and developing varied discourses that will help them to learn effectively in the classroom setting. Consider whether discussing the following strategies may be appropriate for your students.

- Ways of showing that you are listening (examples: looking at the speaker, nodding, responding)
- Ways of indicating that you do not understand (examples: "I don't know;" "I don't understand.")
- Ways to get another child's attention or the attention of a group (examples: "Excuse me;" "May I have your attention?")
- Ways to join a conversation or activity (examples: playing alongside; raising a hand or finger when in a group; asking "May I join you?")
- Ways to invite others to participate in conversations or activities (examples: "Would you like to...?" "What are you thinking?")
- Ways to solve conflicts that arise while working together in small groups
- Ways of considering whether you have done your "best work"
- Ways of working with or requesting support from other students

To support children in developing these classroom discourses, brainstorm lists of ideas with the children that you may refer back to over the course of the year. Working with children to develop these lists rather than treating the children as the audience for such conversations will respect their diverse linguistic practices and make space for those practices to become a resource for classroom learning.

2

Shared Reading:
An Assessment-Based Approach

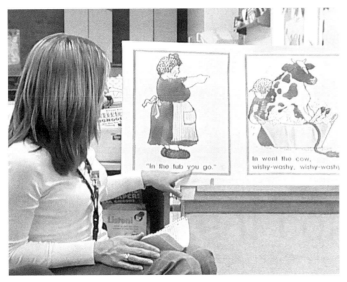

"In the tub you go."

In went the cow, wishy-washy, wishy-washy

CONSIDER THE RESEARCH: In the early childhood classroom, shared reading provides a unique and useful context for supporting children's literacy development. Shared reading supports children's motivation to read, as well as their comprehension of the materials read, alphabet recognition, sense of print directionality, phonemic awareness, phonics knowledge, phonological processing, and familiarity with word forms and phrases (Allington 2006; Ehri and Sweet 1991; Lonigan, 1999; McGee and Morrow 2005; Snudden 1998). Following guidelines suggested by Holdaway (1979), shared reading typically involves children in previewing a text and making predictions with the teacher's support, listening to a skilled reading of the text, discussing the text, and then rereading many times.

This lesson is designed to teach specific procedures and patterns for the shared reading portion of circle time, as well as many reading strategies. It should be taught after children have been familiarized with basic circle routines (Lesson 1).

Form 2.3

Preschool	Kindergarten	First Grade
Encourage during Procedures 1–2:	Encourage during Procedures 1–2:	Encourage during Procedures 1–2:
▪ predicting text content	▪ predicting text content	▪ predicting text content
▪ monitoring meaning	▪ monitoring meaning	▪ monitoring meaning
Choose an instructional focus for Procedure 3:	Choose an instructional focus for Procedure 3:	Choose an instructional focus for Procedure 3:
▪ directionality (use pointer or finger)	▪ directionality (use pointer or finger)	▪ directionality (use pointer or finger)
▪ one-to-one matching of oral or written words (use pointer or finger for one or two sentences—reread a few times)	▪ one-to-one matching of oral and written words (use pointer or finger)	▪ one-to-one matching of oral and written words (use pointer or finger)
▪ predicting words when teacher pauses	▪ predicting words (use Post-its and then uncover onset and rest of word to confirm)	▪ predicting words (use Post-its and then uncover onset and rest of word to confirm)
▪ noticing repetition, rhymes, and alliteration	▪ noticing repetition, rhymes, and alliteration, and using them to support word identification	▪ noticing repetition, rhymes, and alliteration, and using them to support word identification
▪ discussing illustrations and using them to support meaning making	▪ using illustrations to support word identification and meaning making	▪ using illustrations to support word identification and meaning making
▪ alphabet and letter-sound knowledge (locate letters and use Wikki Stix or highlighting tape to mark)	▪ alphabet and letter-sound knowledge (locate letters, sounds, and word families, use Wikki Stix or highlighting tape to mark)	▪ letter-sound knowledge (locate letters, sounds, and word families; use Wikki Stix or highlighting tape to mark)
▪ word knowledge (locate words, repeated words, or words that begin alike and use Wikki Stix or highlighting tape to mark)	▪ word knowledge (locate high frequency, familiar, rhyming, or repeated words and use Wikki Stix or highlighting tape to mark)	▪ word knowledge (locate high frequency, familiar, rhyming, or repeated words, and use Wikki Stix or highlighting tape to mark)
▪ predicting what a word might be based on the first letter	▪ analyzing unknown words (blending by sound or chunk, trying different sounds)	▪ analyzing unknown words (blending by sound or chunk, trying different sounds)
▪ reading holistically (using what is remembered from previous reading in combination with own insights and use of print and picture cues)	▪ monitoring meaning and cross-checking using meaning, structure, and word cues	▪ monitoring meaning and cross-checking using meaning, structure, and word cues
▪ reading expressively	▪ reading with fluent phrasing and expression	▪ reading with fluent phrasing and expression

Form 2.3 Teaching Tool: Shared Reading Focus for Instruction Chart

7 4

Form 2.3

Teaching Tool: Shared Reading Focus for Instruction Chart

Shared reading involves three procedures:

1. *Teacher and students preview text and predict its content.*
2. *Teacher reads aloud and leads a discussion about the content.*
3. *Teacher and students read together several times, using the opportunity to study various reading strategies.*

Depending on the length of the text, you may implement all three of the shared reading procedures on a given day, or you may implement Procedures 1 and 2 on the first day and reserve Procedure 3 for subsequent days.

▪ Hang the circle time routine list from Lesson 1 (Form 1.1) on the wall.

▪ Select a focus for instruction for Procedure 3 (see Form 2.3 for grade-level suggestions).

▪ Select or create a large-print text that would work well for teaching the focus strategy. Because working toward fluency is a goal of shared reading, the same text may be used for up to a week. Nursery rhymes, poems, and big books with predictable story lines or predictable language work well. If necessary, make transparencies to enlarge the text. The text you use early on will set the stage for what children think they can do. Starting with short, catchy text that children quickly memorize helps them to see reading as something they can do. Many of the texts you use should have illustrations so that children can explore the ways illustrations connect with the author's words. Form 2.1 provides some rhymes to use as starters. Form 2.2 provides a list of texts that may be used throughout the year, with grade-level suggestions.

▪ You also may need:

- a pointer for children to track text
- Post-its to cover some of the words in the text
- Wikki Stix (commercially produced wax-covered yarn) or cardboard "word frames" to frame words
- highlighting tape to mark words or word features.

INTRODUCTION

Procedure 1. *Lead the children to preview the text (title, author, illustrations) and make predictions about the content.*

EXAMPLE

Literature: **Mrs. Wishy-Washy**

Focus for Procedure 3: **Predicting and confirming unknown words**

After the circle time greeting and calendar review, refer to the circle routine hanging on the wall (Form 1.1) and signal that it is time for shared reading. Show the text.

❝First, I'll read this to you and then we'll read it together a few times. The title is *Mrs. Wishy-Washy. [Point to title.]* Joy Cowley is the author. *[Point to author.]* The first part of shared reading is always to preview the text. Let's do that: What does the cover of this book tell you—what do you predict the book might be about? Look at the illustration. Does it tell you anything about this character? What is she doing? What could the title mean?"

❝Readers **think** like this! They preview a book cover before they read it, and really start to think about what's going to be inside."

❝The next part of shared reading is just to listen. Listen, and let's see how your predictions hold up."

continued

MODELING AND SCAFFOLDING

Procedure 2. *Read the text aloud to the children (all the way through one or two times depending on length) and discuss it with them in a way that fosters their enjoyment and comprehension.*

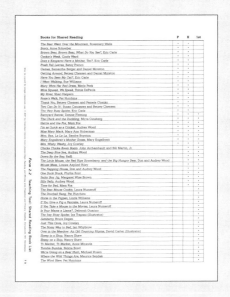

Jack, be nimble,

Jack, be quick,

Jack, jump over

The candlestick.

Form 2.1a–h

Teaching Tool: Mother Goose Rhymes for Shared Reading

Form 2.2

Teaching Tool: Shared Reading Book List

EXAMPLE cont.

Read aloud, discussing content as appropriate.

" How did your predictions hold up? What do you think about the ending?"

continued

Procedure 3. *Read the text aloud with the children over the course of three to five days. Allow a child to track the print with the pointer on some of the readings. Implement a particular focus for instruction (see Form 2.3).*

EXAMPLE cont.

*To prepare for teaching the strategy of **predicting and confirming unknown words**, quickly place a Post-it over three words in the text:* jumped, rolled, paddled.

" I have covered three words in the text. *[Show.]* When we get to them, we'll predict what they are and then we will check under the Post-it to be sure we are correct."

As you come to each word, uncover the first letter to confirm or disconfirm the prediction. For example:

" The first letter is a *J*. You predicted *jumped*. Does the *J* tell you that you might be correct? Let's look at the rest of the word just to be sure."

" So, when you see a word you don't know, you can predict what it might be. And you can look at the first letter and the rest of the word to confirm that you are correct."

CLOSURE

"What did you learn about reading today?"

*-----

CENTER ACTIVITY

The texts used for shared reading should be available to students *(preferably at an easel)* as a daily center or choice activity. See Lesson 9 for procedures for introducing shared reading as a center activity.

kidWATCHING:

Use Form 2.4 to help determine the concepts to focus on during shared reading. Use Form 2.4 to plan instruction that is based on your assessment of children's needs.

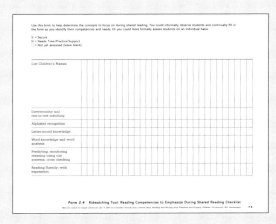

Form 2.4
Kidwatching Tool: Reading Competencies to Emphasize During Shared Reading Checklist

Read-Aloud:

Procedures and Early Comprehension Strategy Instruction

CONSIDER THE RESEARCH: Research shows that not only do read-alouds develop children's reading interest and motivation, but they also lead to improved vocabulary, sense of story, understanding of text structures, and skill in decoding and comprehending (Armbruster, Lehr, and Osborn 2001; Braunger and Lewis 2006; Bus, Van Ijzendorn, and Pellegrini 1995). When preparing for a read aloud, it's important to preview the literature, so that you may thoughtfully discuss it and model your ways of interpreting it. Previewing is also important because it enables expressive reading (changes in volume, pitch, speed, and voices for characters). Listening to a text read expressively increases children's satisfaction and shows them how a reader interprets an author's meaning (Opitz and Rasinski 1998).

This lesson is designed to teach specific procedures for exploring comprehension strategies during the read-aloud portion of circle time. **Day 1** of the present lesson shows the language a teacher might use to introduce the formal procedures for the read-aloud—probably after a week or two of school—and **Day 2 and Beyond** provides an example of what the first two to three weeks (or longer) might look and sound like. The present lesson is used to begin comprehension strategy instruction, and should be implemented daily until Book 2 Lesson 1 (Expanding the Read-Aloud: Building Strong Comprehenders from the Start) is introduced.

PREPARATION

- Hang the circle time routine list from Lesson 1 (Form 1.1) on the wall.

- Prepare Form 3.2 to use as a visual. Or take a photograph of a student engaged in each activity and use the photographs for visuals.

- Select a thinking strategy (Form 3.1) to model and scaffold. Form 3.1 offers a set of thinking strategies to be used early in the year. Teach each for a week or more. Any effort you make here will prepare children for the more complex attention to comprehension processes introduced in Book 2—*Building, Energizing, and Re-envisioning the Literacy Curriculum.*

- Choose an engaging piece of literature that would work well for teaching the strategy. You may wish to read the entire text through on one day before using it to instruct in thinking strategies the next day. This will depend on the length of the text and on the thinking strategy you are teaching. Some strategies work well on a first read while some are easier to teach on a second read.

Teacher Read-Aloud

Talk and listen.

Think like a reader.

Form 3.2
Classroom Visual: Teacher Read-Aloud

INTRODUCTION – Day 1

After the circle time greeting, calendar review, and shared reading, use Form 1.1 to signal that it is time for the read-aloud.

"We are going to do something a little different starting today. As we do our read-aloud, you will probably learn the most and enjoy it the most if we all do two things. Let me show you what they are, and we'll try them together." *[Refer to Form 3.2 for each component of the modeling and scaffolding.]*

MODELING AND SCAFFOLDING – Day 1

Talk and Listen:

"Many times during the day, we're all talking or reading at the same time, but read-alouds are a time when you'll learn most if we have more of a conversation. Let's try it right now. The title of this book is _____, and the author is _____. Look at the cover of this book and think about what it will be about." *[With nonfiction: what you think you might learn.]*

"**Let's talk and listen** to one another about this." *[Encourage children to respond to one another's thoughts rather than engaging in a conversation.]*

"Another way to **talk and listen** is to discuss something with the person next to you. Quietly tell the person next to you what you think this book will be about. You should both take a turn."

Think Like a Reader:

"Readers are always thinking—about what might happen next, and about other things, too…and that's the other thing we'll do. When we read together, we'll **think like readers.** As I read every day, I will stop two or three times to show you some different ways readers think, and I'll ask you to talk about what you are thinking. Today we're going to be stopping and thinking about _____."

Model and scaffold using one of the thinking strategies in Form 3.1, offering many opportunities for students to talk and listen. Some teachers find it helpful to use Post-its to mark where they want to model, and jot down what they want to say.

CLOSURE – Day 1

"It helps us learn when we think and talk about books like we just did. What was it like to follow our procedures *[refer back to Form 3.2]*? How do you think they helped you learn?"

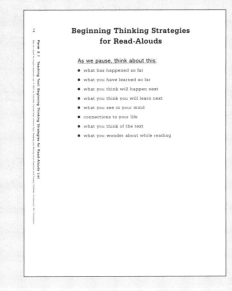

Form 3.1
Teaching Tool: Beginning Thinking Strategies for Read-Alouds List

Use this form to help determine the concepts to emphasize as you support children's participation and engagement in circle experiences.

S = Secure
N = Needs Time/Practice/Support
☐ = Not yet assessed (leave blank)

List Children's Names

Typically sits and
listens attentively

Talks about books and
listens to others

Engages with text and thinks
like a reader

For children who do not participate attentively or effectively, consider doing the following.

- Set up an agreement for the children to attempt five minutes of high-quality participation before moving to another activity (Play-Doh, book bin, or drawing). Extend to ten, fifteen, and twenty minutes.
- Enlist the children's help in choosing the literature to be read for a week of read-alouds.
- Use book possibilities suggested on an interest inventory (see Book 2 Form 5.2: Interest Inventory).
- Enlist the children's help in modeling the "think topics" during the class read aloud by prereading parts of the upcoming book together.
- Try new or unexpected genres such as game instructions for classroom games or humorous poetry.
- Have a week of small-group read-alouds for the children with whom you are concerned. Emphasize and scaffold effective participation.
- Explore what happens with changes in seating position.
- Direct conversation directly to the child who has had difficulty, involving him or her in the conversation.
- Show the chart above and ask the child to self evaluate. For areas that need improvement, discuss ideas to try.

Form 3.3 Kidwatching Tool: Participation and Engagement in Circle Experiences Checklist

May be copied for single classroom use. © 2007 by Gretchen Owocki from *Literate Days: Reading and Writing with Preschool and Primary Children.* Portsmouth, NH: Heinemann.

Form 3.3

Kidwatching Tool: Participation and Engagement in Circle Experiences Checklist

kidWATCHING:

After a few days, you may wish to use Form 3.3 to organize your observations and plan minilessons as needed. Use this form for a few weeks until you move more deeply into strategy instruction. When the more in-depth strategy instruction begins, you may wish to switch to Form 1.7 (Individual Evaluation of Comprehension Strategies) in Book 2 *Building, Energizing, and Re-envisioning the Literacy Curriculum.*

EXAMPLE: DAY 2 AND BEYOND

After introducing the read-aloud on Day 1, implement the following format for several weeks — until Book 2 Lesson 1 is introduced. For each lesson, you will need to select a piece of literature and a thinking strategy (as listed on Form 3.1).

Literature: **Little Red Riding Hood (Trina Schart Hyman)**

Thinking Strategy: **What has happened so far**

Introduction

After the circle time greeting, calendar review, and shared reading, signal that it is time for the read-aloud.

" Remember, as we do our read-aloud, you will probably learn the most and enjoy it the most if we all do two things." *[Review Form 3.2 and refer to it for each component of the modeling and scaffolding.]*

" Today, to **think like a reader**, we are going to stop every so often to think about **what has happened so far**. That's what readers do; we really try to track what is happening in a story. That helps us to talk about it and understand it well."

Modeling and Scaffolding

" Look at the cover of this book and think about what it will be about. Let's **talk and listen** to one another about this." *[Encourage conversation among children rather than a back-and-forth with you only.]*

" Okay, now let's **think like readers** by stopping every so often to think about what has happened so far. As I read, I will stop to show you how I do this and then I'll ask you to do it, too."

continued

EXAMPLE: DAY 2 AND BEYOND cont.

After reading through page 7 of Little Red Riding Hood:

❝Let me stop here to show you how I think about what has happened so far. I'm going to turn back and use the pictures to help."

Referring to page 1:

❝This is a story about Little Red Riding Hood."

Referring to page 2:

❝One morning her mother gave her a basket to take to her grandma."

Referring to page 6:

❝Little Red Riding Hood met a wolf in the woods."

Referring to page 7:

❝And she talked to the wolf."

After you model one or two times, stop every page or two for the children to try out the strategy in pairs.

Closure

❝When we read or listen to a book, it helps us learn when we think and talk about it like we just did. What was it like to stop and retell? How do you think this helps you learn?"

EXTENSION

After a few read-aloud sessions, introduce some early literature response activities that involve drawing and writing. These will change as you move into more depth with your comprehension instruction (Book 2 Lessons 1 *(Expanding the Read-Aloud: Building Strong Comprehenders from the Start)* and 2 *(Using Literature Response as a Tool for Supporting the Development of Content and Literacy Knowledge))*, but use the early days of school to give students a general feel for written and drawn responses. The following are suggested topics for the first few weeks of school. To the extent possible, relate the response experience to the thinking strategy. For example, if you have modeled the thinking strategy of "thinking through what has happened so far," use the response time to draw and write about something such as one key event in the story. (Afterward, at a whole-class meeting, all of the children could be guided to put their events in a meaningful order.)

- Draw one of the characters and write something about that character.
- Draw and write something the author taught.
- Draw and write about something you found interesting.
- Draw and write about something you liked.
- Draw and write about a key event.
- Draw and write about a connection to your life.

Writing Workshop:
Building a Foundation from Which Writers Can Grow

CONSIDER THE RESEARCH: To make your writing workshop successful and enjoyable from the start, introduce it with an emphasis on drawing. Until children develop control over several conventions of written language, their drawings are likely to carry their meaning more effectively than their writing (Graves 1983; Kress 1997). In addition, drawings are more accessible to peers than writing, and therefore elicit more responses. Although we may eventually expect more writing than drawing (for kindergarten and first-grade students), drawing remains important because it continues to give children ideas for writing, expand their thinking on a topic, and help them hold images and ideas in their minds.

This lesson (implemented over the course of a few weeks or much longer for younger students) is designed to teach children the routines and expectations for writing workshop, and to get them started writing in a collaborative setting.

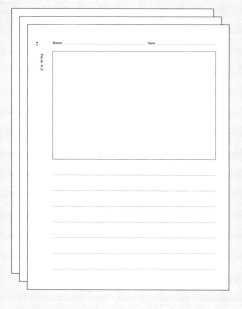

Forms 4.2, 4.3, 4.4, 4.5
Lined Paper Templates

Beginning Ideas for Drawing and Writing in a Workshop Setting

Draw something:

- about you.
- about someone in your family.
- you have done outside of school.
- you have seen outside of school.
- you like to do.
- you don't like to do.
- you do often.
- you would like to try.
- you have just learned how to do.
- you have just learned about.
- you have done at school so far.
- you have seen at school so far.
- special that has happened to you.
- your family does often.
- you like to play.
- you like to imagine.

Form 4.1
Teaching Tool: Beginning Ideas for Drawing and Writing in a Workshop Setting List

PREPARATION

- Prepare for the lesson each day by gathering a stack of plain paper, a red folder (for finished work) and a green folder (for work in progress) for each child, and a can of sharp pencils.

- In place of plain paper, you may wish to use varied forms of lined paper. (See Forms 4.2, 4.3, 4.4, and 4.5.)

Note to preschool and kindergarten teachers:

- As needed, also provide a name card for each student.

- Do not be concerned if children do not show interest in referring back to items placed in the green folder, or if they want to place all documents in the red folder. The process involved in the writing and drawing may be much more meaningful than the product. Toward the latter half of kindergarten, the green folder may take on more significance.

INTRODUCTION

Bring the children to sit together in the place where group meetings occur.

"Every day, we're going to meet here to share ideas about writing, and then you'll have a chance to try out the ideas we talk about. Today, we'll begin: I am going to give you a plain piece of paper and something to try out."

MODELING

As children watch, write your name and the date on the paper, and read aloud what you have written. In the interest of time and focus, teach children to use numbers for dates — or provide date stamps.

"Please do what I did: write your name and the date. Then please draw _____. [Offer a prompt from Form 4.1.] What might you draw? I might draw _____. [Articulate the main idea of your drawing.] When you have finished drawing, please write something about your picture."

EXTENSION

Teach students to reserve the first line on Forms 4.2–4.5 for a title.

The prompts provided in Form 4.1 are meant to be starter examples. Develop and extend as you get to know your students, and also offer open-ended prompts such as, "just write today," "try a story," "write about something real," or "write something you see someone in your family write."

"Please sit at your table as you work. I will come around to see what you are doing. I will want to talk with you about your work because that will help me know how I can teach you best. In ten or twenty minutes, we will come back here and you may share your work." *[Have each student pick up a piece of paper and a pencil. Encourage a talk-filled, collaborative atmosphere as the students work.]*

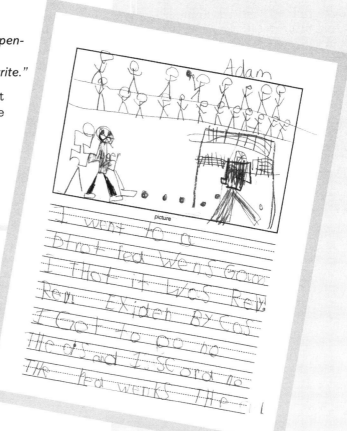

SCAFFOLDING

The following scaffolding prompts are designed to support them in showing you what they know and can do.

- **Encourage personally meaningful content** so that children are not drawing and writing just because they have to, but instead, to reflect on and share important information: *"What did you do? What did you see? How did you feel? Draw/write that."*
- **Encourage detail:** *"Tell me more. Then what happened? What else happened? What did it look like? What did it sound like? Draw/write that."*

kidWATCHING:

Use the first weeks of school to learn as much as you can about your students as people and as writers. Pay attention to what they do when you prompt them to articulate the content or main ideas in their drawings. Observe and document the quality of children's engagement and participation in the workshop experience so that you can tailor your instruction to meet their specific needs in this area. Form 4.6 may be useful.

- *To students who indicate they **do not know how to write their names**, respond without surprise, saying, "Yes, then you will write the first letter, and I will help you to do that right now." Referring to the child's name card, coach the child to write as much as necessary to copy the first letter—and more if it seems appropriate. "Pick up your name card every day and do what we just did."*

- *To students who indicate they **do not know how to draw,** respond without surprise, saying: "Then you can learn by making marks on the paper. Just play around with making marks. That is the way to learn."*

- *To students who indicate they **do not know how to write,** respond without surprise, saying: "Tell me about your picture." If the child expresses little detail, prompt for more. When you get more detail, say: "Write that!" Show with your demeanor your expectation that the child can write. If the child does not write, repeat what she has said, and then show your expectation that she will write it. If the child still does not write, help her to listen for the sounds in the first few words and then encourage her to proceed independently. You may find it easier to encourage labeling before sentence-writing, but either is appropriate to encourage from the start.*

- *To students who indicate they **do not know what to write or draw,** refer back to the prompt(s). As a last resort, ask specific questions: "Do you like to…? Have you ever…?"*

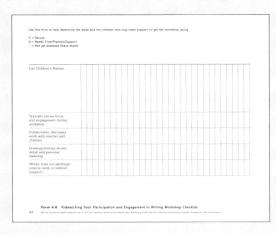

Form 4.6
Kidwatching Tool: Participation and Engagement in Writing Workshop Checklist

CLOSURE

"What did you draw and write today? Who would like to share? If you are not finished and would like to work on your piece again tomorrow, please take your green folder. If you are finished with your piece, and would like to start fresh tomorrow, please take your red folder." *Hand each child a folder. Students place their papers in the folder, and then place the folders in a designated storage area.*

Re-envisioning the Alphabet Curriculum

CONSIDER THE RESEARCH: An important goal for preschool and kindergarten children is that they learn to recognize letters effortlessly. Letter knowledge (when measured at the beginning of kindergarten) is a well-established and reliable predictor of later reading achievement (Bond and Dykstra 1967; Scanlon and Vellutino 1996; Strickland and Shanahan 2004), probably because letter naming serves as a mediator for remembering and working with sounds (IRA/NAEYC 1998). The National Association for the Education of Young Children (NAEYC) recommends teaching uppercase before lowercase letters, and introducing just a few letters at a time (IRA/NAEYC 1998). Although knowledge of the alphabet is foundational for learning to write and read, children need not know all of the letters in order to begin to do either. Using meaningful literacy experiences to talk about the alphabet is an important way to support children's development.

This set of six lessons is designed to support children's recognition and beginning use of the letters of the alphabet. As these lessons are being taught, children should also be engaging in shared reading, guided reading, independent/paired reading, interactive writing, and independent/collaborative writing experiences because they will learn much about the alphabet through those experiences.

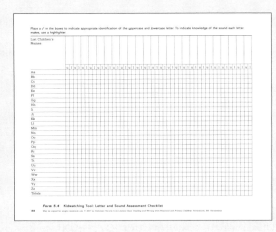

Place a ✓ in the boxes to indicate appropriate identification of the uppercase and lowercase letter. To indicate knowledge of the sound each letter makes, use a highlighter.

Form 5.4 Kidwatching Tool: Letter and Sound Assessment Checklist

Form 5.4

**Kidwatching Tool: Uppercase and
Lowercase Letter Assessment Checklist**

N	D	A	H	R	W	Z
K	O	E	B	I	S	X
U	L	P	F	C	J	T
Y	V	M	Q	G		

n	d	a	h	r	w	z
k	o	e	b	i	s	x
u	l	p	f	c	j	t
y	v	m	q	g		

Form 5.5 Student Tool: Upper and Lowercase Letter Assessment Form

Form 5.5

**Student Tool: Upper and Lowercase
Letter Assessment Form**

PREPARATION

Have available a pointer and piece of chart paper with the alphabet written on it (or have available an enlarged alphabet strip). Additional materials (listed below, within each of the six lessons) will depend on which lesson is being taught.

Avoid letter-of-the-week programs. They are not necessary, and for many children, they are not helpful. When such programs are implemented, some children will already know the letter of the week, and are already using it in their writing and reading. And, all children need more than one letter per week to write and read. Instead of teaching one letter per week, individualize your instruction, and focus on helping all children to develop insight into the letters and sounds that they haven't yet learned. There is no scientific evidence that studying one letter per week, in some special order, works better than focusing on teaching letters and sounds as they are connected to meaningful reading and writing.

Note to first-grade teachers: This lesson is designed primarily for use with preschool and kindergarten students. However, first-grade students who do not recognize letters effortlessly can benefit from these lessons.

Note to kindergarten teachers: Assess your students' letter knowledge (Forms 5.4 and 5.5) before teaching these lessons. Some of the lessons may be more appropriate for small groups who need work with letters than for the entire class. If you have students who do not need work with letters, their time might be more fruitfully spent writing or working with books.

Note to all teachers: As you assess children's letter knowledge and phonics knowledge, keep in mind that children's understandings may more easily reveal themselves implicitly than explicitly. That is, they may be able to use certain knowledge as they read or write, but be unable to consciously articulate it in an isolated assessment situation.

Make it a practice to introduce all alphabet lessons using a format similar to the one that follows.

INTRODUCTION

Every time you teach one of the alphabet lessons, start by using the pointer to lead the children in singing The Alphabet Song.

"We've just used these letters to help us sing The Alphabet Song *[referring to the alphabet chart]*. Now, look around you and find a letter somewhere else in the room. When you find a letter, point to it." *[Select a child.]*

"_____, come with me and point to the letter you have chosen so that everyone can see it." *[Select individual children to use the pointer to show the class the chosen letter. Walk with each child to the letter so that you can help the child point out the letter and trace it with a finger if it is within reach. If the letter is not within reach, you trace the letter with a finger as the children watch.]*

"Who can tell us what this letter is? This is letter _____. Trace this letter in the air with your finger *[Model.]*."

"This letter is part of the word _____. Let's read it together."

MODELING, SCAFFOLDING, AND CLOSURE

Select from the following six lessons, teaching each one as many times as it seems beneficial. Teach the Name Cards lesson first and then vary the order of the rest according to what you think your students might enjoy and benefit from most.

NAME CARDS LESSON

Preparation: Prepare a name card for each child and a blank note card for each child.

"Today I'm going to give you a card with your **name** on it." *[Hand the cards to the children.]*

"Here's a card with *my* name on it. Watch how I point to each letter in my name." *[Point and say letters aloud.]*

continued

Collect a name-writing sample from each child. Place a check or write the date next to each competency the child demonstrates. Use the chart to plan for individualized instruction and mini-lessons, and to track growth over time.

List Children's Names												
No attempt												
Uses squiggles or letter-like symbols												
Uses random strings of letters												
Uses some letters in name (indicate how many: 4/6)												
Conventional spelling of first name with appropriate capitalization												
Conventional spelling of first and last name with appropriate capitalization												

Form 5.3 Kidwatching Tool: Observing Children's Name Writing Checklist

Form 5.3

**Kidwatching Tool: Observing Children's
Name Writing Checklist**

kidWATCHING:

Observe the children carefully as they write their names and take notes that will allow you to pull children into instructional groups that are based on need. For example, for children who write their first names conventionally, form a group to work on last names, or to work on capitalizing the first letter and using lowercase letters for the rest. For children who say they can't write their names, form a group to start working on writing the first letter. You may also wish to form groups for children who need support with letter formation or pencil grip. Form 5.3 may be useful to organize your planning.

NAME CARDS LESSON cont.

❝Now, point to each letter in your name.❞

❝Now, say the letters, if you know what they are.❞ *[Encourage children to do this with a partner.]*

❝Now look closely at those letters before you give your cards to me because I have a challenge. I'm going to take the cards and then give them back to the wrong person! You'll walk around and talk about the letters and see if you can help each other get your own cards back.❞ *[Collect the cards and then hand them back to the children randomly. Engage in this card exchange a few times.]*

■ As the children become familiar with the concept of written names, engage with them in various studies. For example, categorize written names by their beginning letters, beginning sounds, number of syllables, or number of letters.

❝Now I have one more challenge for you. I'm going to give you a blank card and I would like for you to write your name on it. When you are finished writing, please give me your card.❞

■ As the children return their cards to you, say, "Show me what you wrote" or Tell me about this."

WORD CARDS LESSON

Preparation: Prepare a word card for each child. Put a different word on each card. Use the same set of cards for several lessons.

Preschool teachers: Choose words that may serve a purpose in classroom writing and reading, such as: *dear, to, a, love, like, from, I, we, can, see, you, friend, my, by, mom, dad, the, grandma, grandpa, brother, sister.* Or choose words that are part of a theme your class is studying such as: *apple, banana, cherry, grape, kiwi, orange, pear, pineapple.*

continued

Kindergarten and first-grade teachers: Choose words that the children use often in their writing or choose from the word lists provided with Book 2 Lesson 9 (Word Study: Focusing on the Essentials). Or choose words that are part of a theme your class is studying, such as: insect, legs, abdomen, body part, head, thorax, wing, nectar, leaf, plant, life cycle.

" Today I'm going to give you a card with a word on it. Hand the cards to the children, showing the class each word and drawing attention to the first letter (or letters). Think aloud about how looking at the letters could help you read the word. For example, "We're going to be using our fruit cards. Here's one that starts with M *(point to the M)*. M is for mmmm-mango."

■ Keep a card for yourself, to use for modeling.

" I have a card with the word _____ on it. Let me show you the letters." *[Point to and name each letter.]*

" Now, point to each letter in your word. Name the letters, if you know what they are." *[Encourage children to do this with a partner.]*

" Now look closely at the word on your card because I have a challenge. I want you to show the word and tell about it. Maybe you will name some of the letters. Maybe you will name all of the letters. Maybe you know the first sound. Maybe you can read the word."

" Let me show you what I might do with my card." *[Offer many possibilities that are reflective of your students' current knowledge.]*

" Study your word with your partner and get ready to tell us what you know." *[Allow several children to respond, prompting them to talk about the word's features.]*

Center Possibilities

■ Place the cards in a word study center and encourage students to sort them and read them to one another.

■ Hang the set of cards to be visible from the writing table. Encourage students to use the cards as appropriate.

■ Invite children to bring in a label from a piece of environmental print. Make word cards from these and allow children to work with them in a center.

ALPHABET STRIPS LESSON

Preparation: Prepare an alphabet strip for each child (see Form 5.1). Enlarge a strip to be used for modeling. The strips may be taped to tables or desks, or they may be laminated. For the lesson, each child needs a copy of the strip.

■ Pass out the alphabet strips.

"When you are writing, you can use this alphabet strip to help you. All of the letters you need for writing are here. Look at the strip and see if you can find the first letter in your name."

"Let's sing *The Alphabet Song* while I point to each letter on the strip."

"Now let's say the name of each letter on the strip without singing."

"Next, let's look at the pictures and see if you can name each to yourself." *[Point to each one.]*

"Now let's name the pictures together. *A* is for..."

"Finally, how do you think this strip could help you as you are writing?" *[Accept all responses.]*

"As you are working, I will watch over you and see how you are using your strips."

Note: The easiest and most productive way to teach children to use these strips effectively is to do so in context, as they are writing. As you observe, take note of how they are using the strips. You will probably want to repeat this lesson with the whole class several times as you identify their needs in using the alphabet strips.

■ Ask students to share how they used their strips.

Center Possibilities:

Make the strips available at the writing table. Writing and talking about letters will support children's development of alphabet knowledge.

Make the strips available at the word study center.

■ Ask children to read the pictures.

■ Ask children to read the letters.

continued

Form 5.1
Student Tool: Alphabet Strip

ALPHABET STRIPS LESSON cont.

- Show students how to cover about five letters with Post-its. Show them how to guess what the missing letters might be and then check by looking under the Post-it.
- Ask children to read every-other-letter.
- Ask children to read the strip backwards.

LETTER FORMS LESSON

Preparation: Gather enough magnetic letters or letter tiles for children to use in small groups or at a center.

" Today I'm going to give you a basket of letters to play with in a group *[or at a center.]* I would like you to _____ ." *[Select from the list in Form 5-2 and model and talk through what you expect from your students.]*

- Ask students to share what they did with the letters.

Center Possibilities

Students may be encouraged to use center time to engage in any of the activities on the list featured in Form 5.2.

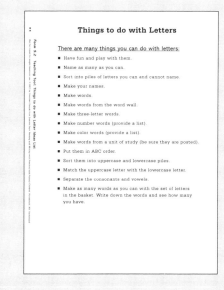

Form 5.2
Teaching Tool:
Things to do with Letters Ideas List

kidWATCHING:

Use Forms 5.4 and 5.5 to assess students' knowledge of letters.

MANIPULATIVES LESSON

Preparation: Have available either Play-Doh, sand, or finger paint.

" Today I would like for you to spend some time making letters from Play-Doh (or sand or finger paint). Let me show you how to roll the dough into strips (or take just enough paint, or prepare a sand tray) so that you can make letters and words."

" Who would like to suggest a word I could write?" *[Take a few suggestions and model how to write in the particular medium. Show children how you could look for letters and words around the room as you work.]*

Center Possibility

■ Set up a center for children to use Play-Doh, sand, or finger paint to write letters and words.

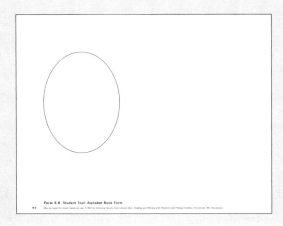

Form 5-6
Student Tool: Alphabet Book Form

ALPHABET BOOKS LESSON

Preparation: You will need one alphabet book.

Note: Regularly reading alphabet books with your students will help them understand the concept of "letter" and will provide opportunities for developing letter-sound knowledge.

- Introduce the book by previewing the cover and the pages. After you preview, go through quickly and say the entire alphabet as you turn through the pages and show the students each letter.

- Read and discuss the book.

Center Possibilities

- Set up a center that includes several alphabet books.

- Create a class alphabet book that involves each child in creating one or two pages. To prepare, write each of the 26 letters lightly on the back of 26 pieces of paper and allow children to choose which page or pages they will illustrate. Use Form 5.6 as a standard form for alphabet books, showing students how to write their letter of choice in the oval space.

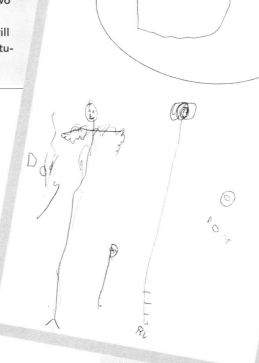

Energizing the Writing Center

CONSIDER THE RESEARCH: Children learn to write by writing (NCTE 2004). Through the act of writing, especially in a social setting, they simultaneously develop many understandings, including: how to form letters, spell words, put spaces between words, use punctuation, form a meaningful message, engage an audience, and use the features of a particular genre (Goodman and Wilde 1992; Graves 1982; 1983; Sulzby 1985). To keep children's learning meaningful, make an effort to support them in exploring these competencies simultaneously. Even preschool students should be encouraged to write varied types of meaningful messages, using the understandings and resources they currently have. Sometimes this means that a random string of letters is a "story" or a squiggly line is a "sign." Support even the youngest children in getting ideas on paper, and you are supporting many critical aspects of their literacy development.

Along with creating general workshop time for writing (Lesson 4), set up an inviting writing table for use during center time. For both experiences, children will need to know how to use the materials. This lesson serves that function. After teaching this lesson, allow the students several weeks for open exploration in the center before moving to Book 2 Lesson 8 (Supporting Genre Exploration Through the Writing Center).

- Neatly organize different types of paper and envelopes on a shelf, and place baskets of writing utensils, tape, and staplers at the table.

- For an introductory lesson, invite the class to sit on the floor near the table. Select three children to serve as models.

INTRODUCTION

"Using this writing table will be one of the choices you have during center time. Today I will show you all of the materials you may choose from so that you may do the kind of writing you enjoy. You may also use these materials during writing workshop."

MODELING

Show students where you keep the crayons, markers, pencils, stapler, tape, envelopes, and paper.

"Let's say that _____ wants to write or draw on **paper**. _____, please choose a piece of paper and bring it to the table. Please write your name first and then you may begin working. Go ahead and get started."

"Let's say that _____ wants to make a **book**. _____, please choose two pieces of paper—the same size—and bring them to the table. Let me show you one way to make a book. *[Guide child to fold the two papers in half and staple along the edge.]* Where would you put the title? Since you are the author, where would you write your name? Please write your name on the front cover."

"Gregory the germ buster" sign

"Let's say that _____ wants to write a **note**. _____, please choose one piece of paper and an envelope and bring them to the table. Whose name should be written on the envelope? *[Discuss possible audiences for notes.]* Please write a name on the envelope."

EXTENSION

As the children become familiar with the materials at the writing center, show them how to use them in new ways. Children especially enjoy making texture books, lift-the-flap books, signs, and various kinds of greeting cards, and they enjoy writing letters and notes to important people in their lives. Use real text models to teach children how to design these types of texts and write in these genres.

"When you are finished at the writing table, please put the crayons, markers, and pencils back in their baskets and check to see that your space is clean. _____, _____, and _____, please show the class how you will do that."

"Then, you have to decide where to put your work. If you want to share something at meeting time, put it on the easel so that we'll remember. If it's something to take home, put it in your bag."

"The writing table has enough chairs for six writers. If ever you find that the chairs are all taken, you may use a clipboard to write somewhere else in the classroom."

SCAFFOLDING

"As you are working this week, I will watch over you to see what you are doing at the writing table and help you learn to use the materials in new ways."

All drawing and writing
- Your name

Drawing
- Labels
- Captions

Books
- Title
- Author
- Cover illustration
- Writing or illustrations

Letters and notes
- Dear ,
- Message or Picture
- Your name

Signs
- Brief message
- Appropriate for wide audience

Greeting cards
- Cover illustration
- Dear
- Message
- Your name
- Envelope names

Form 6.1
Teaching Tool: Emphasizing Genre Characteristics Talking Points

CLOSURE

"Who used the writing table today? What did you write or draw? Where did you put your finished work? Did the area stay neat?"

kidWATCHING:

As your students use the writing center over the course of a few weeks, use Form 6.2 to take note of their activity and to determine the focus of your next teaching efforts.

What are the children doing in the writing center?	What are they talking about?
What might I do to further their exploration of literacy concepts?	What needs my attention?

Form 6.2 Kidwatching Tool: Writing Center Notes
9.2 May be copied for single classroom use. © 2007 by Gretchen Owocki from *Literate Days: Reading and Writing with Preschool and Primary Children*. Portsmouth, NH: Heinemann.

Form 6.2
Kidwatching Tool: Writing Center Notes

Re-imagining the Library Center

CONSIDER THE RESEARCH: In classrooms that have libraries, children read 50 percent more than children in classrooms without libraries (Cullinan and Galda 1998). And many studies have shown that the more children read, the higher their reading achievement (Anderson, Wilson, and Fielding, 1988; Elley 1992; Mullis, Campbell, and Farstrup 1992). Regardless of how many children's books you have, use them to form a classroom library, and give your students the time and support they need to read with engagement in that library. Even a set of fifty books is enough to get started. As your children read, make a conscious effort to help them develop and articulate their tastes and preferences. "Intelligent readership depends upon...informed judgements and tastes..." (Kohl 1999, p.3).

This lesson is designed to teach children to select, use, and replace classroom library books.

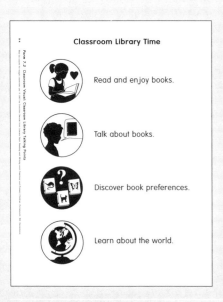

Form 7.1
Classroom Visual: Library Labels

Form 7.2
Classroom Visual:
Classroom Library Talking Points

PREPARATION

- Arrange your classroom library books into three sections: fiction, nonfiction, and poetry. Along with this, create special bins for books grouped by author (red bins) and topic (blue bins). If desired, photocopy and laminate the Classroom Library Labels (Form 7.1) for your bookshelves and bins. The **Topic** and **Author** labels provide a space for writing which topics and authors the bins contain.

- Select four children to serve as models.

- Prepare Form 7.2 as a visual.

Note to preschool teachers: You may wish to limit the possibilities to fiction, nonfiction, and poetry rather than introducing the topic and author bins right away. When your students are accustomed to this organization, add one bin at a time for topics and/or authors.

INTRODUCTION

Bring the children to the classroom library to sit in a circle on the floor.

"Look around you and think for a moment. What would you like to do in this space?" *[Work with children to raise each talking point on Form 7.2.]*

- Read and enjoy books.
- Talk about books.
- Discover book preferences.
- Learn about the world.

"Today, we'll discuss how to get started doing these things. All of these will help you get better and better at reading."

MODELING

"When you are in the library, you may use any of the books. Let me show you how they're organized so you can find the ones you want."

"The books in red bins are grouped by **who wrote them**. *[Show 2-3 sets.]* The author name is on the bin. The books in blue bins are grouped by **topic.** *[Show 2-3 sets.]* The topic name is on the bin."

"The rest of the books are on three shelves. This shelf is for **storybooks**—or **fiction** *[show two or three]*; this shelf is for **books about real things**—or **nonfiction** *[show two or three]*; and this shelf is for **poetry** *[show two or three]*. The labels will help you remember. Let's read the labels together *[fiction, nonfiction, poetry]*."

To the four models:

"Please go choose a book you think you might enjoy—and try to remember where it came from. Then, sit anywhere: on the beanbag chair, the couch, or the rug; far apart or right next to each other."

"When you use the library, you may read by yourself or you may read and talk with others. Please, always use a soft-talking voice, like I am using right now—just so we can all hear one another. Let's all say *hello* in a soft-talking voice to see what that feels like."

"When you are finished with a book, please put it back where you found it—in a bin or on one of the three shelves. Why do you think we do this? Show us how to put a book back in the place you found it."

SCAFFOLDING

"As you use the library today, please do these things *[refer back to each item on the visual]*. When you are finished with a book, return it to its place. I will watch over you today to help you."

Note to preschool teachers: Spend lots of time in the library, reading books as children request it and talking through the ideas in books with them. This will familiarize the children with the contents of the books in your library, and with the close-up actions of a proficient reader. Use this opportunity daily to put your arm around a child, to hold someone's hand, and to give someone your undivided attention.

Form 7.3
Kidwatching Tool:
Classroom Library Notes

Form 7.4
Kidwatching Tool:
Book Preferences Notes

CLOSURE

" Who enjoyed a book? Which books did you enjoy? Who learned something? What was it like to use a soft-talking voice? Was it easy to return the books to the same place you found them?"

kidWATCHING:

As your students use the library over the course of a few weeks, use Form 7.3 to take note of their activity and to determine where to focus your teaching efforts next.

kidWATCHING:

Use Form 7.4 to take note of the books your students particularly enjoy. This will help you to support them in identifying and discussing their preferred topics, authors, and genres. Draw from the list you create as you select literature to be used for whole-class or small-group instruction.

EXTENSION

Model for students how to use Post-its to record what you are learning and thinking about as you read books. Place a pad of Post-its in the library so that children may use them as they are reading.

Taking Full Advantage of the Listening Center

CONSIDER THE RESEARCH: Use a listening center throughout the year. Research shows that listening to a text while following along with the print enhances comprehension, develops fluency, and supports children's development of the skills and strategies that support word identification (Opitz and Rasinski 1998). In addition, the more texts children listen to, the more exposure they have to vocabulary and concepts about the world—and these are critical to comprehending the wide body of content children will encounter throughout their early years of schooling.

Teach children procedures for using the listening center, and teach variations of listening experiences to try throughout the year. You may wish to change the listening center activity every three to six weeks in order to keep children appropriately challenged. However, if you never change the activities and just allow them to listen, the center will still be quite beneficial.

PREPARATION

- Start the school year with a listening area that includes tape recorders and headphones. Collect tapes with matching versions of printed text (stories, poetry, and nonfiction), or create the tapes yourself. If you have multiple copies of some texts, you may wish to start with these; this will give you time to develop the collection. Depending on how you use the center, you may also wish to have blank tapes available.

- To introduce the center, select one of the listening experiences listed in Form 8.1. Bring the students to sit on the floor near the listening center to show them what is expected. Use this center throughout the year, introducing new listening experiences over time.

- Select four students (or as many as will be working in the center) to serve as models.

The activities are ordered according to approximate difficulty. It is recommended that you start at the top of the list, and if you have younger students allow them more time to explore each.

Preschool, Kindergarten, Grade 1

Allow students to engage in the following for 3-6 weeks each — or longer:

- Listen to the tape and enjoy the illustrations.
- Listen to the tape and then draw something you learned.
- Listen to the tape and then draw something you found interesting.
- Listen to the tape. As you listen, draw pictures about what you are hearing.
- Listen to the beginning of a story and draw how you think it will end.
- Listen to the tape and then use a retelling guide (Form 8.2 or 8.3) to retell it with your group or partner.
- Listen to the tape and then (using Form 8.4 or 8.5) rethink it by drawing and writing with your group or partner.

Kindergarten, Grade 1

- Listen to the tape and follow along with the printed text. As you listen, read aloud using a soft voice.
- Listen to the tape and follow along with the printed text. Turn off the tape recorder and read the same text aloud with a partner.
- Listen to the tape and follow along with the printed text. Read the same text aloud to a partner, and then listen to a partner read it.
- Choose one of the texts at the table and read it aloud into the recorder. Listen to the recording.
- Choose one of the texts at the table and practice reading it aloud into the recorder. Listen to the recording, thinking about how to read more expressively. Tape yourself again.

Form 8.1
Teaching Tool:
Listening Experiences Ideas List

INTRODUCTION

❝What good books have you *listened* to lately? Today I want to show you something to try at the listening center."

The first time you teach this lesson, show the children how to use the listening equipment, and then use child models to walk through pressing the buttons themselves. The children's performance will give you an idea of how much support will be needed at the center during the first weeks.

MODELING

Support the child models as they quickly walk through the procedures involved with carrying out one of the activities listed in Form 8.1. Rather than focusing on literacy teaching per se in this phase of the lesson, focus on helping the students to understand what they are expected to do in terms of procedures. An example of language to use for modeling follows:

Have available a pad of Post-its.

"For the next few weeks you'll be listening to nonfiction books—books about real things. After you listen to these books, I would like you to draw something the author taught. Our four models here are going to show us what this might look like. You each need one Post-it and a copy of the book that will be in the tape player."

"I'll read aloud the first part while you follow in your copy. When you hear something interesting the author is teaching, place your Post-it right there in your copy so that you remember what you want to draw on it. Let's try it."

Begin reading. If students do not use the Post-its within the first few pages, prompt them to think about what the author is teaching and to mark an interesting part with the note. Show them how to remove a Post-it from an earlier page and move it to a later page if they decide to change their original plans.

"When the tape ends, use your Post-it to draw something the author taught."

SCAFFOLDING

Visit the center daily to observe and scaffold the children's literacy activity. Focus on supporting them in following along with the text, reading fluently, and responding to the content of the books they have listened to.

CLOSURE

"Who used the listening center today? Did the equipment work okay? How did you do when you were following along with the text? How did you do with _____ (the drawing, the writing, the retelling, the rethinking, the reading aloud, or the practice reading)? How do you think this helps you learn?"

Form 8.6
Kidwatching Tool: Listening Center Notes

kidWATCHING:

As your students use the listening center, regularly evaluate their literacy activity. Use Form 8.6 to take note of their activity and to determine where to focus your teaching efforts next.

Building Reading and Writing Skill at the Easel Center

CONSIDER THE RESEARCH: Children learn by interacting with the knowledge of their culture *as it is being used* (Dewey 1897). Just as they learn to talk by talking, and to draw by drawing, they learn to read and write by engaging in real acts of reading and writing. Sometimes teachers think of literacy centers as a place for children to only *practice* skills and strategies that have been taught, rather than a place to develop significant new competencies. But that's not how learning works. Developmental psychologists and reading scholars have taught us that reading and writing knowledge are constructed by *the teacher within* — as that teacher socially participates in activities valued by the culture (Bredekamp and Copple 1997; Ferreiro and Teberosky 1982; Piaget 1952; Vygotsky 1978). A key role for teachers is to ensure that their students have many rich opportunities for focused reading and writing both with and without immediate teacher presence.

This lesson is designed to teach children procedures for shared reading and interactive writing at the easel center.

45

PREPARATION

As you are planning center or choice activities, right from the start, include an easel that children may use for shared reading and interactive writing. Use this center throughout the year.

Setting up for shared reading at the easel center: After you have modeled the shared reading process (as in Lessons 1 and 2) make the text available at the easel center (along with a pointer) for children to read together. Allow them to use Wikki Stix, word frames, and highlighting tape, as appropriate (as in Lesson 2).

Setting up for interactive writing at the easel center: After you have modeled any kind of writing on large chart paper (drawing on students to help you with ideas, formatting, spelling, or punctuation, as in Lesson 11), have large paper available for children to use to model for and write interactively with one another.

INTRODUCTION

Bring the children to sit on the floor near the easel (where the easel center will be located).

"I want to do something special with you: play school! You'll have lots of chances to do this when you use this center. Who would like to be the teacher right now? _____, will you please pretend to be the teacher so we can generate some ideas for what the pretend teacher and the students could do at the easel center?"

MODELING

Shared Reading: Show the students the big books and other large-print texts they may use to read together. Invite the child serving as model to use a pointer to guide the class in reading, and to use the Wikki Stix, word frames, and highlighting tape, as appropriate.

EXAMPLE OF MODELING TO SUPPORT SHARED READING

"You have lots of big books and charts to choose from when you play here. _____, could you please choose a big book and sit in the teaching chair?"

"Think about the first thing we do when we read a big book together. What would a teacher do before reading? *[Encourage students to discuss ways of previewing the text, including looking at the cover, looking through the pages, and making predictions.]* _____, go ahead and lead us in a preview of the text."

"Now let's think about the different ways we read big books together."

Encourage students to consider the following choices: teacher reads; teacher and children read together; teacher reads, using pointer for the first few pages; child reads, using pointer for the first few pages; two children read together.

"_____, choose a way and let's read."

"Think about what we do after we read a big book together. The first thing I always ask is, "What did you think about while I was reading this?" _____, go ahead and ask!"

"Then, the last thing we usually do is study something in the book—like letters, or sounds, or word families. Let's think through how we do this. *[Encourage students to discuss ways of studying concepts through shared reading, as listed in Form 2.3.]* _____, can you think of something you'd like us to study? Go ahead. Let's try it."

"What we've just done is one way to play at the easel center. When you read books here, I'd like you to preview first, then think of a way to read, then talk about the book, and then study something in the book. Have fun today!"

Interactive Writing: Show the students the paper and markers they may use to engage in their own interactive writing. Invite the child serving as model to write a sentence interactively with the class.

What are the children doing in the easel center?	What needs my attention?
Which children need extra support or accommodations to effectively engage with print in this center?	What kinds of support or accommodations do they need?

Form 9.1 Kidwatching Tool: Easel Center Notes

Form 9.1
Kidwatching Tool: Easel Center Notes

kidWATCHING:

As your students use the easel center, regularly take note of what they are doing with reading and writing. Use Form 9.1 to take note of their activity and to determine where to focus your teaching efforts next.

EXAMPLE TO SUPPORT INTERACTIVE WRITING

❝When you play school here, you may write on the chart paper. If you are the teacher, you should first decide what you are going to write. What are some of the things we write on chart paper when I am teaching you (e.g. lists of words, notes, stories, nonfiction information)? When you are the teacher, you could choose to write any of these things."

❝Do you notice that when I write on chart paper, I am always teaching you something about writing or drawing? If you are the teacher, you should also have something in mind to teach. What are some of the things I teach as we write together (e.g. spelling, word spacing, punctuation, adding detail to a drawing)?"

❝_____, what would you like to write with us? What could you teach as you do this? Go ahead. Let's try it."

❝What we've just done is one way to play at the easel center. When you write here, if you are the teacher, I'd like you to be sure to teach something about writing. Have fun today!"

SCAFFOLDING

Support creativity and playfulness. As you visit this center early on, encourage students to engage in shared reading and interactive writing, but allow them to extend what you have modeled and explore new possibilities. Early on, help them to understand the general format and procedures for child-led reading and writing at the easel. As they become more confident and independent, participate as a "student," contributing ideas and knowledge as the "teacher" allows or requests it.

CLOSURE

❝Who read something in the easel center today? Who wrote something? What did you read and write? How do you think your work in the easel center helps you with your learning?"

Using the Play Center to Facilitate Literacy

CONSIDER THE RESEARCH: Theory and research link play with myriad aspects of child development, including literacy (Johnson and Christie 2000). Play is an ideal medium for fostering literacy because it: provides a setting that promotes literacy exploration; builds on prior literacy knowledge; develops language; highlights the connections between oral and written expression; develops abstract thinking (a requirement for working with the symbols of the alphabet); is a place where children feel free to take risks; and provides rich opportunities for teaching (Bruner 1983; Pellegrini and Galda 1993; Roskos and Christie 2001; Roskos and Neuman 1993; Schrader 1989, Vukelich 1991; Vygotsky 1978).

> Support children in using literacy materials to enhance their play. Introduce one to two new literacy props per week.

PREPARATION

- Start the school year with a "home living" area that includes literacy props such as pads of paper and pencils, children's literature, a telephone book, a recipe book, a television guide, a newspaper, and food packaging. Add props over time.

INTRODUCTION

"I want to show you some of the materials in the play center so you'll have lots of ideas for what you could do here. Has anyone seen or used one of these? *[Hold up literacy objects from the center.]* How do families use this?"

MODELING

Children serve as powerful literacy models for one another, but take time each day to visit the center and model at least one use of written language. Focus your modeling on themes the students are already exploring. For example, if they are turning the center into a restaurant, sit down and say, "Oh, we need a menu." List and sketch a picture of the actual play foods you have in the center. If they are planning a birthday party, sit down and sketch an invitation.

SCAFFOLDING

As children are playing, look for meaningful ways to scaffold: to encourage and support literacy uses and behaviors. For example, encourage children to read a menu, providing a bit of support as they read or attempt to read it. Or support a child to write some words on a party invitation.

CLOSURE

"Who read something in the play center today? Who wrote something? What did you read and write? Are there any more materials that we might want to add? Here's something I saw _____ do." *[Show and explain the actual material the child read or wrote.]*

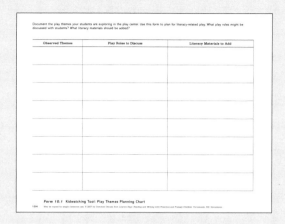

Form 10.1
**Kidwatching Tool:
Play Themes Planning Chart**

kidWATCHING:

Take note of the play themes your students are developing out of the home living center (such as shopping, caring for babies, law enforcement, or operating a restaurant). Use Form 10.1 to record your students' play interests and to plan for literacy-related play.

11

Interactive Writing:
Focus on Spelling

CONSIDER THE RESEARCH: Early childhood teachers are responsible for seeing that their students learn to spell more and more words conventionally. Encouraging children to "try out" spellings is one key to achieving this goal because it forces consideration of the relationships between sounds and letters, it leads to thinking about spelling patterns and principles, and it often inspires collaboration with peers. "Trying it out" also allows children, as they are learning to spell conventionally, to explore all of the other concepts and processes (such as how to format a piece, how to engage an audience, and how to choose a good topic) that are involved with meaningful writing.

Use interactive writing to teach many writing skills and strategies, introducing **spelling** early in the year. The present lesson teaches children to think through a spelling. Although the present lesson focuses on spelling only, it is easily adapted to model numerous other strategies for writing, such as the ones listed on Form 11.1.

Interactive writing involves the teacher acting as scribe while modeling and seeking student input on the use of the strategy.

PREPARATION

Implement interactive writing lessons regularly as part of the writing workshop minilesson, or give interactive writing its own time slot on several days of the week (for example, at 9:55 on the example schedule featured in Form TG-10 in the Teacher's Guide).

- Determine a topic and genre for interactive writing. Choose a topic related to the content curriculum, and a genre related to what you are teaching your students in writing workshop (such as captions, labels, letters or notes, a personal narrative, a story, or a description). In all cases, choose meaningful content and a genre that your students are already exploring—or likely to explore soon.

You may wish to purchase individual white boards for each student to use during interactive writing lessons. This allows each child to actively explore the strategies you are teaching, and gives you some important opportunities to kidwatch.

Strategies for Writing

- word spacing (preschool, kindergarten, first grade)
- working with a focused topic in drawing or writing (preschool, kindergarten, first grade)
- adding details or captions to a drawing (preschool, kindergarten, first grade)
- developing a character in writing or drawing (preschool, kindergarten, first grade)
- sequencing a set of drawings or a piece of writing (preschool, kindergarten, first grade)
- creating a meaningful setting through writing or illustrations (preschool, kindergarten, first grade)
- formatting a piece of text (preschool, kindergarten, first grade)
- punctuating (kindergarten, first grade)
- adding details to a piece of writing (kindergarten, first grade)
- creating rich beginnings and endings (kindergarten, first grade)
- writing a topic sentence (first grade)

Form 11.1
Teaching Tool:
Strategies for Writing Ideas List

INTRODUCTION

"Over the next week we are going to be writing _____ *[mention topic and/or genre]*. When you are writing, lots of you have been asking me how to spell all kinds of words. Today, I want to work on solving some spellings together so that you can get used to doing this on your own as you write."

MODELING

"Let's say I want to write _____."

*For a lesson on spelling, just one or two sentences will suffice. Or you could write a list, or captions or labels for a picture, or a short note. Model your thought processes about **spelling only** rather than a broad variety of writing concepts.*

Think aloud as you write the sentence, focusing on showing students how you use spelling strategies such as listening for sounds in words or consulting the word wall.

Before writing some words, ask students to try them out on their own (on the white boards) first. Seek student input as you write the words on your paper, but when the pen is in your hand, spell all words conventionally (correctly). If student suggestions are incorrect, acknowledge the sensibility of their choices but spell the word conventionally. Explain that children need to "try out" and write their own spellings so that they can do all kinds of writing, but it will take time to learn to spell like an adult.

Note to preschool teachers: Take most of the responsibility for the spelling but request student input on initial consonants or on familiar names.

Note to kindergarten teachers: Allow children to spell many of the words, but not to the extent that they become restless and distracted by the activity. Encourage students to listen for and include all of the sounds in words, and take note of word spelling patterns (common word families) that might warrant a specific minilesson (see Extension activity on next page).

Note to first-grade teachers: Give most of the responsibility for the spelling to the students. Support them with complex spelling patterns, and take note of spelling patterns (common word families) that might warrant a specific mini-lesson (see Extension activity on next page). If you have words on a word wall, use this opportunity to refer students there for spellings.

Form 11.2
**Kidwatching Tool:
Considering Developmental Phases
of Spelling Checklist**

Form 11.2 Kidwatching Tool: Considering Developmental Phases of Spelling Checklist
106   May be copied for single classroom use. © 2007 by Gretchen Owocki from Literate Days: Reading and Writing with Practice and Purpose (Owocki, Portsmouth, NH: Heinemann)

kidWATCHING:

Collect a few writing samples from each student
to reflect on the individualized spelling instruction
you will provide. Use Form 11.2 to identify where
students fall, and then aim your instruction at their
likely next step (as indicated on the chart).

EXTENSION

As a part of interactive writing, give impromptu or planned minilessons focused on words and word families. For example as a class, you could make a list of words starting with a certain onset (such as *t, sh,* or *l*) or ending with a certain rime (such as *–op* or *–ate*). Or as you list words that rhyme, you might sort by spellings (*-ait, -ate, -eat*) and discuss which spellings seem to be used most often for a particular sound. As a center activity, students might make their own lists or sort the words from a list the class has generated.

SCAFFOLDING

"As you are writing today, listen for sounds and try out any spellings you need. Talk with one another about spellings! I will watch over you so see how you are doing."

CLOSURE

"What is a word you tried out today?"

"How did you figure out how to spell it?"

Using Names as a Tool for Literacy

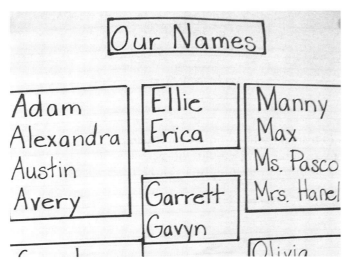

CONSIDER THE RESEARCH: Because children's written names are personally significant and encountered repeatedly, they are a particularly useful tool for teaching. Exploring names sensitizes children to the concept of *letter* and *word,* provides them with alphabet knowledge, and helps them learn about letter-sound relationships. Research shows that very young children who can write their names show similar progress in other areas of literacy: letter knowledge, word knowledge, rhyme awareness, beginning sound awareness, and awareness of the functions of print (Bloodgood 1999; Welsch 2003). It is typical for young children to begin writing their names with a scribbled line, and then move to shapes that look like letters before using conventionally formed letters (Welsch 2003). Names are often the first words that children learn to spell conventionally.

This lesson involves children in studying their own and others' names—as a route to developing insights into various concepts about print.

PREPARATION

- Place Post-its and pencils at a table to be used as a sign-in station. Nearby, hang a piece of chart paper for children to put their Post-its on.

Note to preschool and kindergarten teachers: Print each child's name on a note card. (Some will prefer to copy their names and will find it easier to copy from a single-name model on the table than from a distant model that contains many names.) Also create a classroom word wall just for the children's names.

- Select three children whose signatures look very different (in terms of development) to serve as models. Invite the class to sit on the floor near the table.

INTRODUCTION

"I need your help. I need to keep track of who is here every day, but I'm usually doing other things in the morning. Tomorrow, would you please write your name on a Post-it when you come in and put it on this chart? Then we can quickly see who is here."

MODELING

"_____, will you please show us how you will do this tomorrow when you come in?"

Go through this process with three children. Accept all developmental forms as name writing (zigzag lines, shapes that look like letters, letter strings). To children who indicate they do not know how to write their names, respond without surprise, saying, "Yes, then you will write the first letter, and I will help you to do that right now." *Referring to the name card, coach the child as much as necessary to copy the first letter—and more if it seems appropriate.*

SCAFFOLDING

"As you come in tomorrow, we'll have Post-its and pencils on this table. I will watch over you as you write your name and put it on the chart, and I'll help with whatever you need. Right now, I'll give you a Post-it to practice. Take it to your table, write your name, and place it on the chart. Then sit down and we'll discuss how it worked."

EXTENSION

As your students come in one day, use the opportunity to teach them to take their own lunch count. For example, pink Post-its could be used by those who brought a lunch and yellow by those who are going to eat a school lunch. Or start a process of using a certain color to represent the daily helper.

CLOSURE

"Let's look at our chart. I see that you have all written your names. How did this go today? Was anything hard about it?"

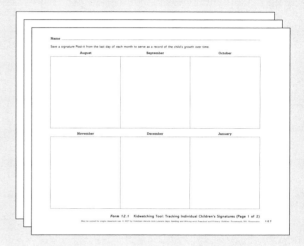

Form 12.1
Kidwatching Tool:
Tracking Individual Children's Signatures

kidWATCHING:

Use Form 12.1 to save a Post-it from the last day of each month. Use this record to discuss growth over time both with children and their families.

EXTENSION

As the children become familiar with the concept of written names, engage with them in various "studies." For example, categorize written names by their beginning letters, beginning sounds, number of syllables, or number of letters.

EXTENSION

Whenever appropriate, use *wait lists* as a way to get children reading one another's names. For example, wait lists could be created for computer use, daily helpers, or to gain access to a special center.

BOOK EXTENSION

Read *Chrysanthemum* (Henkes). Send each child home with a half-page note to parents: At school, we are talking about names this month. How did you choose my name? Or what is special about my name or names?

Appendix

Circle Time Routine

1. Greeting

2. Calendar

1	2	3	4	5
6	7	8	9	10	11	12
13	14	15	16	17	18	19
20	21	22	23	24	25	26
27	28	29	30	31

3. Shared Reading

Sun House

4. Read-Aloud

Form 1.1 **Classroom Visual: Circle Time Routine**

Children Who Don't Seem Engaged	Possible Reasons	Strategies for Improvement

Form 1.2 **Kidwatching Tool: Circle Time Notes**

Jack, be nimble,

Jack, be quick,

Jack, jump over

The candlestick.

Form 2.1a   Teaching Tool: Mother Goose Rhymes for Shared Reading

To market, to market,

To buy a fat pig.

Home again, home again,

Jiggety jig.

Form 2.1b Teaching Tool: Mother Goose Rhymes for Shared Reading

There was an old woman,

Who lived under a hill.

And if she's not gone,

She lives there still.

Diddle, diddle, dumpling, my son John,

Went to bed with his stockings on.

One shoe off and one shoe on,

Diddle, diddle, dumpling, my son John.

Bat, bat,

Come under my hat,

And I'll give you a slice of bacon.

And when I bake,

I'll give you a cake

If I am not mistaken.

Hey diddle, diddle, the Cat and the Fiddle,

The Cow jumped over the Moon;

The little Dog laughed to see such sport,

And the Dish ran away with the Spoon.

Form 2.1f Teaching Tool: Mother Goose Rhymes for Shared Reading

Pease porridge hot,

Pease porridge cold,

Pease porridge in the pot,

Nine days old.

Some like it hot,

Some like it cold,

Some like it in the pot,

Nine days old.

There was a crooked man,

Who walked a crooked mile.

He found a crooked sixpence,

Against a crooked stile.

He bought a crooked cat,

That caught a crooked mouse,

And they all live together,

In a little crooked house.

Books for Shared Reading

Books for Shared Reading	P	K	1st
The Bear Went Over the Mountain, Rosemary Wells	*	*	
Boots, Anne Schreiber	*	*	
Brown Bear, Brown Bear, What Do You See?, Eric Carle	*	*	
Cookie's Week, Cindy Ward	*	*	
Does a Kangaroo Have a Mother, Too?, Eric Carle	*	*	
Fresh Fall Leaves, Betsy Franco	*	*	
Games, Samantha Berger and Daniel Moreton	*	*	
Getting Around, Betsey Chessen and Daniel Moreton	*	*	
Have You Seen My Cat?, Eric Carle	*	*	
I Went Walking, Sue Williams	*	*	
Mary Wore Her Red Dress, Merle Peek	*	*	
Mice Squeak, We Speak, Tomie DePaola	*	*	
My River, Shari Halpern	*	*	
Rosie's Walk, Pat Hutchins	*	*	
Thank You, Betsey Chessen and Pamela Chanko	*	*	
Two Can Do It!, Susan Canizares and Betsey Chessen	*	*	
The Very Busy Spider, Eric Carle	*	*	
Barnyard Banter, Denise Fleming	*	*	*
The Chick and the Duckling, Mirra Ginsberg	*	*	*
Hattie and the Fox, Mem Fox	*	*	*
I'm as Quick as a Cricket, Audrey Wood	*	*	*
Miss Mary Mack, Mary Ann Hoberman	*	*	*
Moo, Baa, La La La, Sandra Boynton	*	*	*
Mary Engelbreit's Mother Goose, Mary Engelbreit	*	*	*
Mrs. Wishy Washy, Joy Cowley	*	*	*
Chicka Chicka Boom Boom, John Archambault and Bill Martin, Jr.		*	*
The Deep Blue Sea, Audrey Wood		*	*
Down By the Bay, Raffi		*	*
The Little Mouse, the Red Ripe Strawberry, and the Big Hungry Bear, Don and Audrey Wood		*	*
Mouse Mess, Linnea Asplind Riley		*	*
The Napping House, Don and Audrey Wood		*	*
One Duck Stuck, Phyllis Root		*	*
Sailor Boy Jig, Margaret Wise Brown			*
Silly Sally, Audrey Wood		*	*
Time for Bed, Mem Fox		*	*
The Best Mouse Cookie, Laura Numeroff			*
The Doorbell Rang, Pat Hutchins			*
Horse in the Pigpen, Linda Williams			*
If You Give a Pig a Pancake, Laura Numeroff			*
If You Take a Mouse to the Movies, Laura Numeroff			*
Is Your Mama a Llama?, Deborah Guarino			*
The Itsy Bitsy Spider, Iza Trapani (Illustrator)			*
Jamberry, Bruce Degen			*
Just This Once, Joy Cowley			*
The Noisy Way to Bed, Ian Whybrow			*
Over in the Meadow: An Old Counting Rhyme, David Carter (Illustrator)			*
Sheep in a Shop, Nancy Shaw			*
Sheep on a Ship, Nancy Shaw			*
To Market, To Market, Anne Miranda			*
Tumble Bumble, Felicia Bond			*
We're Going on a Bear Hunt, Michael Rosen			*
Where the Wild Things Are, Maurice Sendak			*
The Wind Blew, Pat Hutchins			*

Form 2.2 **Teaching Tool: Shared Reading Book List**

Preschool	Kindergarten	First Grade
Encourage during Procedures 1–2:	**Encourage during Procedures 1–2:**	**Encourage during Procedures 1–2:**
■ predicting text content ■ monitoring meaning	■ predicting text content ■ monitoring meaning	■ predicting text content ■ monitoring meaning
<u>Choose an instructional focus for Procedure 3:</u>	<u>Choose an instrc3uctional focus for Procedure 3:</u>	<u>Choose an instructional focus for Procedure 3:</u>
■ directionality (use pointer or finger)	■ directionality (use pointer or finger)	
■ one-to-one matching of oral or written words (use pointer or finger for one or two sentences—reread a few times)	■ one-to-one matching of oral and written words (use pointer or finger)	■ one-to-one matching of oral and written words (use pointer or finger)
■ predicting words when teacher pauses	■ predicting words (use Post-its and then uncover onset and rest of word to confirm)	■ predicting words (use Post-its and then uncover onset and rest of word to confirm)
■ noticing repetition, rhymes, and alliteration	■ noticing repetition, rhymes, and alliteration, and using them to support word identification	■ noticing repetition, rhymes, and alliteration, and using them to support word identification
■ discussing illustrations and using them to support meaning making	■ using illustrations to support word identification and meaning making	■ using illustrations to support word identification and meaning making
■ alphabet and letter-sound knowledge (locate letters and use Wikki Stix or highlighting tape to mark)	■ alphabet and letter-sound knowledge (locate letters, sounds, and word families; use Wikki Stix or highlighting tape to mark)	■ letter-sound knowledge (locate letters, sounds, and word families; use Wikki Stix or highlighting tape to mark)
■ word knowledge (locate words, repeated words, or words that begin alike and use Wikki Stix or highlighting tape to mark)	■ word knowledge (locate high frequency, familiar, rhyming, or repeated words and use Wikki Stix or highlighting tape to mark)	■ word knowledge (locate high frequency, familiar, rhyming, or repeated words, and use Wikki Stix or highlighting tape to mark)
■ predicting what a word might be based on the first letter	■ analyzing unknown words (blending by sound or chunk; trying different sounds)	■ analyzing unknown words (blending by sound or chunk; trying different sounds)
■ reading holistically (using what is remembered from previous reading in combination with own insights and use of print and picture cues)	■ monitoring meaning and cross-checking using meaning, structure, and word cues	■ monitoring meaning and cross-checking using meaning, structure, and word cues
■ reading expressively	■ reading with fluent phrasing and expression	■ reading with fluent phrasing and expression

Form 2.3 **Teaching Tool: Shared Reading Focus for Instruction Chart**

Use this form to help determine the concepts to focus on during shared reading. You could informally observe students and continually fill in the form as you identify their competencies and needs. Or you could more formally assess students on an individual basis.

S = Secure
N = Needs Time/Practice/Support
☐ = Not yet assessed (leave blank)

List Children's Names																													
Directionality and one-to-one matching																													
Alphabet recognition																													
Letter-sound knowledge																													
Word knowledge and word analysis																													
Predicting; monitoring meaning using cue systems; cross checking																													
Reading fluently; with expression																													

Form 2.4   **Kidwatching Tool: Reading Competencies to Emphasize During Shared Reading Checklist**

Beginning Thinking Strategies for Read-Alouds

As we pause, think about this:

- what has happened so far

- what you have learned so far

- what you think will happen next

- what you think you will learn next

- what you see in your mind

- connections to your life

- what you think of the text

- what you wonder about while reading

Form 3.1   Teaching Tool: Beginning Thinking Strategies for Read-Alouds List

Teacher Read-Aloud

Talk and listen.

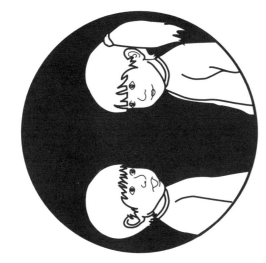

Think like a reader.

Form 3.2 Classroom Visual: Teacher Read-Aloud

Use this form to help determine the concepts to emphasize as you support children's participation and engagement in circle experiences.

S = Secure
N = Needs Time/Practice/Support
☐ = Not yet assessed (leave blank)

List Children's Names																										
Typically sits and listens attentively																										
Talks about books and listens to others																										
Engages with text and thinks like a reader																										

For children who do not participate attentively or effectively, consider doing the following:

- Set up an agreement for the children to attempt five minutes of high-quality participation before moving to another activity (Play-Doh, book bin, or drawing). Extend to ten, fifteen, and twenty minutes.
- Enlist the children's help in choosing the literature to be read for a week of read-alouds.
- Use book possibilities suggested on an interest inventory (see Book 2 Form 5.2: Interest Inventory).
- Enlist the children's help in modeling the "think topics" during the class read aloud by prereading parts of the upcoming book together.
- Try new or unexpected genres such as *game instructions* for classroom games or *humorous poetry*.
- Have a week of small-group read-alouds for the children with whom you are concerned. Emphasize and scaffold effective participation.
- Explore what happens with changes in seating position.
- Direct conversation directly to the child who has had difficulty, involving him or her in the conversation.
- Show the chart above and ask the child to self evaluate. For areas that need improvement, discuss ideas to try.

Form 3.3 **Kidwatching Tool: Participation and Engagement in Circle Experiences Checklist**

Beginning Ideas for Drawing and Writing in a Workshop Setting

<u>Draw something:</u>

- about you.

- about someone in your family.

- you have done outside of school.

- you have seen outside of school.

- you like to do.

- you don't like to do.

- you do often.

- you would like to try.

- you have just learned how to do.

- you have just learned about.

- you have done at school so far.

- you have seen at school so far.

- special that has happened to you.

- your family does often.

- you like to play.

- you like to imagine.

Form 4.1 Teaching Tool: Beginning Ideas for Drawing and Writing in a Workshop Setting List

Name _____

Date _____

Form 4.2

Name

Date

Form 4.3

Use this form to help determine the areas and the children who may need support to get the workshop going.

S = Secure
N = Needs Time/Practice/Support
☐ = Not yet assessed (leave blank)

List Children's Names																								
Typically shows focus and engagement during workshop																								
Collaborates; discusses work with teacher and children																								
Drawing/writing shows detail and personal meaning																								
Writes; tries out spellings/ invents (with or without support)																								

Form 4.6 **Kidwatching Tool: Participation and Engagement in Writing Workshop Checklist**

Aa Bb Cc Dd Ee Ff Gg Hh Ii

Jj Kk Ll Mm Nn Oo Pp Qq Rr

Ss Tt Uu Vv Ww Xx Yy Zz

fox

Form 5.1   **Student Tool: Alphabet Strip**

Things to do with Letters

There are many things you can do with letters:

- Have fun and play with them.

- Name as many as you can.

- Sort into piles of letters you can and cannot name.

- Make your names.

- Make words.

- Make words from the word wall.

- Make three-letter words.

- Make number words (provide a list).

- Make color words (provide a list).

- Make words from a unit of study (be sure they are posted).

- Put them in ABC order.

- Sort them into uppercase and lowercase piles.

- Match the uppercase letter with the lowercase letter.

- Separate the consonants and vowels.

- Make as many words as you can with the set of letters in the basket. Write down the words and see how many you have.

Form 5.2   Teaching Tool: Things to do with Letter Ideas List

Collect a name-writing sample from each child. Place a check or write the date next to each competency the child demonstrates. Use the chart to plan for individualized instruction and mini-lessons, and to track growth over time.

List Children's Names																													
No attempt																													
Uses squiggles or letter-like symbols																													
Uses random strings of letters																													
Uses some letters in name (indicate how many: 4/6)																													
Conventional spelling of first name with appropriate capitalization																													
Conventional spelling of first and last name with appropriate capitalization																													

Form 5.3   **Kidwatching Tool: Observing Children's Name Writing Checklist**

Place a ✓ in the boxes to indicate appropriate identification of the underlined uppercase and lowercase letter. To indicate knowledge of the sound each letter makes, use a highlighter.

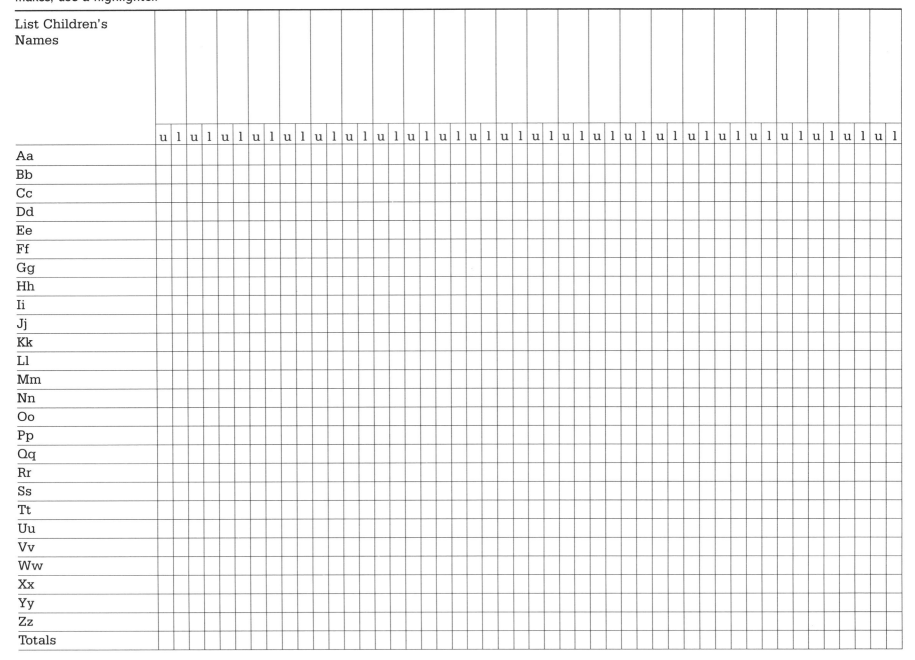

Form 5.4 Kidwatching Tool: Letter and Sound Assessment Checklist

N	D	A	H	R	W	Z
K	O	E	B	I	S	X
U	L	P	F	C	J	T
Y	V	M	Q	G		

n	d	a	h	r	w	z
k	o	e	b	i	s	x
u	l	p	f	c	j	t
y	v	m	q	g		

Form 5.5   **Student Tool: Upper and Lowercase Letter Assessment Form**

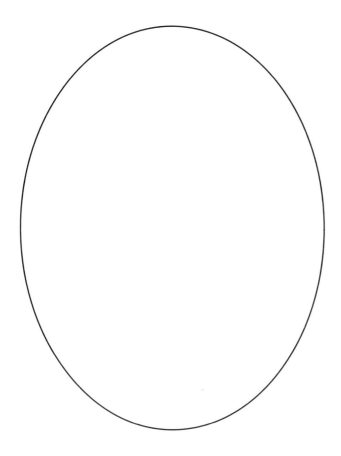

Form 5.6 **Student Tool: Alphabet Book Form**

May be copied for single classroom use. © 2007 by Gretchen Owocki from *Literate Days: Reading and Writing with Preschool and Primary Children*. Portsmouth, NH: Heinemann

All drawing and writing

- Your name

Drawing

- Labels
- Captions

Books

- Title
- Author
- Cover illustration
- Writing or illustrations

Letters and notes

- Dear ,
- Message or Picture
- Your name

Signs

- Brief message
- Appropriate for wide audience

Greeting cards

- Cover illustration
- Dear ,
- Message
- Your name
- Envelope names

Form 6.1 **Teaching Tool: Emphasizing Genre Characteristics Talking Points**

What are the children doing in the writing center?	What are they talking about?
What might I do to further their exploration of literacy concepts?	**What needs my attention?**

Form 6.2 **Kidwatching Tool: Writing Center Notes**

Classroom Library Labels

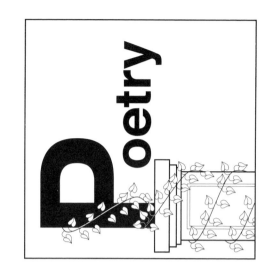

Form 7.1   **Classroom Visual: Library Labels**

Classroom Library Time

Read and enjoy books.

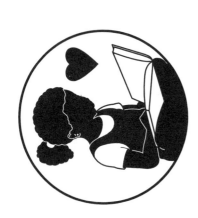

Talk about books.

Discover book preferences.

Learn about the world.

Form 7.2 **Classroom Visual: Classroom Library Talking Points**

What are the children doing in the library?	What needs my attention?
Which children need extra support to engage with books?	**What kinds of extra support might work?**

Form 7.3   **Kidwatching Tool: Classroom Library Notes**

Keep this form in the classroom library. When you observe a child in your classroom particularly enjoying a book, take note. This will help you to support your students in identifying preferred topics, authors, and genres. Draw from this list as you select literature to be used for whole-class or small-group instruction.

Children's Names	Favored Book Titles	Author	Genre

Form 7.4 **Kidwatching Tool: Book Preferences Notes**

The activities are ordered according to approximate difficulty. It is recommended that you start at the top of the list, and if you have younger students allow them more time to explore each.

Preschool, Kindergarten, Grade 1

Allow students to engage in the following for 3-6 weeks each—or longer:

- Listen to the tape and enjoy the illustrations.

- Listen to the tape and then draw something you learned.

- Listen to the tape and then draw something you found interesting.

- Listen to the tape. As you listen, draw pictures about what you are hearing.

- Listen to the beginning of a story and draw how you think it will end.

- Listen to the tape and then use a retelling guide (Form 8.2 or 8.3) to retell it with your group or partner.

- Listen to the tape and then (using Form 8.4 or 8.5) rethink it by drawing and writing with your group or partner.

Kindergarten, Grade 1

- Listen to the tape and follow along with the printed text. As you listen, read aloud using a soft voice.

- Listen to the tape and follow along with the printed text. Turn off the tape recorder and read the same text aloud with a partner.

- Listen to the tape and follow along with the printed text. Read the same text aloud to a partner, and then listen to a partner read it.

- Choose one of the texts at the table and read it aloud into the recorder. Listen to the recording.

- Choose one of the texts at the table and practice reading it aloud into the recorder. Listen to the recording, thinking about how to read more expressively. Tape yourself again.

Form 8.1 **Teaching Tool: Listening Experiences Ideas List**

Retelling Guide for Fiction

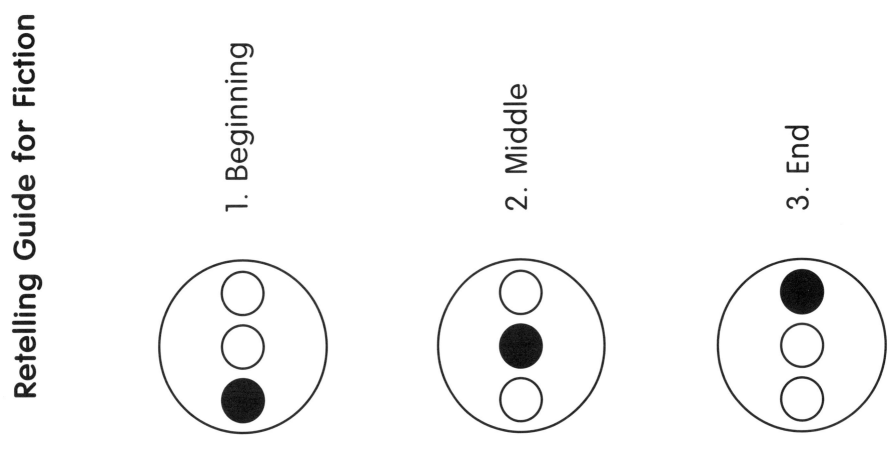

1. Beginning

2. Middle

3. End

Form 8.2 Classroom Visual: Listening and Retelling Guide for Fiction

Retelling Guide for Nonfiction

Topic

What the author taught

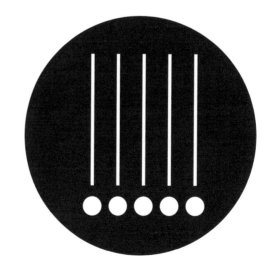

Form 8.3 Classroom Visual: Listening and Retelling Guide for Nonfiction

Rethinking Fiction

Beginning	Middle	End

Form 8.4 Student Tool: Listening to and Rethinking Fiction

Rethinking Nonfiction

Topic:
What we learned:

What are the children doing in the listening center?	What needs my attention?
Which children need extra support or accommodations to read and follow along with the text?	What kinds of support or accommodations do they need?

Form 8.6 **Kidwatching Tool: Listening Center Notes**

What are the children doing in the easel center?	What needs my attention?
Which children need extra support or accommodations to effectively engage with print in this center?	What kinds of support or accommodations do they need?

Form 9.1   Kidwatching Tool: Easel Center Notes

Document the play themes your students are exploring in the play center. Use this form to plan for literacy-related play. What play roles might be discussed with students? What literacy materials should be added?

Observed Themes	Play Roles to Discuss	Literacy Materials to Add

Form 10.1 **Kidwatching Tool: Play Themes Planning Chart**

Strategies for Writing

- word spacing (preschool, kindergarten, first grade)

- working with a focused topic in drawing or writing (preschool, kindergarten, first grade)

- adding details or captions to a drawing (preschool, kindergarten, first grade)

- developing a character in writing or drawing (preschool, kindergarten, first grade)

- sequencing a set of drawings or a piece of writing (preschool, kindergarten, first grade)

- creating a meaningful setting through writing or illustrations (preschool, kindergarten, first grade)

- formatting a piece of text (preschool, kindergarten, first grade)

- punctuating (kindergarten, first grade)

- adding details to a piece of writing (kindergarten, first grade)

- creating rich beginnings and endings (kindergarten, first grade)

- writing a topic sentence (first grade)

Form 11.1 **Teaching Tool: Strategies for Writing Ideas List**

Collect two or three writing samples from each child. Place a check next to each competency the child demonstrates. Use the chart to plan for individualized instruction and minilessons, and to track growth over time.

List Children's Names																										
Uses random strings of letters (*talking* = HLiLL)																										
1–2 prominent sounds represented (*talking* = TK)																										
Most sounds represented (*talking* = token)																										
Demonstrates knowledge of spelling patterns (such as *-ing, -ain, -est, -ed*) (*talking* = toking)																										
Beginning to conventionally spell many commonly used words																										
Most commonly used words are spelled conventionally																										

Form 11.2 **Kidwatching Tool: Considering Developmental Phases of Spelling Checklist**

Name _____

Save a signature Post-it from the last day of each month to serve as a record of the child's growth over time.

August	September	October

November	December	January

Form 12.1   **Kidwatching Tool: Tracking Individual Children's Signatures (Page 1 of 2)**

Name _____

Save a signature Post-it from the last day of each month to serve as a record of the child's growth over time.

February	March	April

May	June	July

Form 12.1 **Kidwatching Tool: Tracking Individual Children's Signatures (Page 2 of 2)**